HEART ATTACK, CARDIAC CATH, AND BYPASS:

A Nurse's Guide to Caring for the Patient

Jillian Riske, MSN, RN-BC, PCCN
Kate Culver, MSN, RN, PCCN

Cover created by Katie Swaim Design

For permission request, write to the publisher as listed below.
Nurseology Consultants LLC
www.nurseology.com
info@nurseology.com

Printed in the United States of America.
ISBN 13: 978-0-9981114-1-4
ISBN 10: 0-9981114-1-4

Ordering Information
Quantity sales: Special discounts are available on quantity purchases by corporations, associations, and others. For details, contact the publisher at the above email address.

Disclaimer
The information provided herein is stated to be truthful and consistent, in that any liability, in terms of inattention or otherwise, by any usage or abuse of any policies, processes, or directions contained within is the solitary and utter responsibility of the recipient reader. Under no circumstances will any legal responsibility or blame be held against the publisher for any reparation, damages, or monetary loss due to the information herein, either directly or indirectly.

The information herein is offered for informational purposes solely, and is universal as so. The presentation of the information is without contract or any type of guarantee assurance.

The trademarks that are used are without any consent, and the publication of the trademark is without permission or backing by the trademark owner. All trademarks and brands within this book are for clarifying purposes only and are owned by the owners themselves, not affiliated with this document.

CONTENTS

About the Authors 6

Preface 8

Chapter 1: Anatomy and Physiology 9

    The Coronary Arteries..9

    The Anatomy of the Heart.......................................10

    The Electricity of the Heart 13

    Cardiac Rhythms 16

Chapter 2: Assessment 18

    Risk Factors..18

    Symptoms of a Heart Attack 19

    Assessment..19

    EKG..20

    Cardiac Enzymes 22

Chapter 3: Initial Treatment 24

    Your patient has developed chest pain. What do you do

    next? 24

    The Next Phase of the Intervention 26

    Fibrinolytics 26

Chapter 4: Cardiac Cath..28

    Precath Care and Orders 28

    The Procedure..29

    Postcath Care and Orders..33

    Femoral Approach..33

    Bedrest 33

    Sheath Care..35

    Sheath Removal 35

    Complications...37

Radial Approach 39
Postcath Orders 39
Chapter 5: Non-STEMI and Unstable Angina 41
Orders 41
Chapter 6: Bypass 45
Preoperative Care and Orders 45
The Surgery 47
Postoperative Care and Orders 49
Complications 53
Chapter 7: Case Studies 55
Case Study 1 55
Case Study 2 56
Case Study 3 57
Conclusion 59
References 60

ABOUT THE AUTHORS

JILLIAN RISKE, MSN, RN-BC, PCCN, completed her B.S. in nursing from the University of Texas at Austin and her M.S. in nursing administration at the University of Texas at Arlington. Jillian has been working in health care for over 10 years. She started as a patient care and monitor technician while in nursing school. After school, she transitioned to her role as a critical care nurse where she found a passion caring for cardiac and neuro patients. She has served in various roles that include bedside nurse, preceptor, charge nurse, and supervisor. Jillian has also taught classes on critical care and cardiac topics.

Early in her career, Jillian completed a specialty nurse fellowship through the hospital where she is employed. Through this fellowship, she implemented the use of a sepsis-screening tool that led to earlier detection of sepsis in patients. She went on to present her findings in a poster presentation at the American Association of Critical Care Nurses National Conference in Washington, D.C. Through her work in the fellowship, she was recognized with a professional contribution award.

Jillian is a member of the American Association of Critical Care Nurses and a past member of Sigma Theta Tau. She holds various certifications in her specialty, including progressive care and board certification.

Jillian resides in Austin, Texas, where she and her husband raise their two young boys. She continues to enjoy bedside nursing and plans to continue writing books to help nurses better understand how to care for their patients.

Publication: Abstract for National Teaching Institute Creative Solutions, poster published in *Critical Care Nurse Journal:* Riske, J. & Butz, M. (2010). CS42 A New Screening Strategy Detects Sepsis and Prevents Septic Shock. *Crit Care Nurse,* 30.

KATE CULVER, MSN, RN, PCCN, has been in health care for nearly a decade. While attending Nursing School at the University of Oklahoma, she worked as a patient care technician in a hospital. After graduating with her B.S. in nursing in 2008, she moved to Austin, Texas, where she began working as a graduate nurse for a well-known hospital organization in the cardiac and intermediate care setting. During her 5 years as a staff nurse, she gained experience in the specialty through a fellowship program, precepting new hires, and charge nursing. Through these experiences and the support of nursing leadership, Kate was able to obtain her progressive care nursing certification.

Eventually, Kate returned to school to obtain her master's of science in nursing administration degree and teaching certificate from the University of Texas at Arlington. After graduating in 2012, she gained experience as a nurse educator in the critical care, orthopedic, and neuroscience specialties. During that time, she was given the opportunity to create simulation scenarios for the hospital partnership's new hire nurses, conduct lectures on critical care and stroke-related topics, validate competencies in nursing skills, and become certified in teaching both basic and advanced cardiac life support classes. This is when her love for teaching was fostered and why she wants to continue contributing to the nursing profession through education. Kate currently works as a nurse manager in the acute care setting on units that primarily care for the neuroscience and orthopedic patient population.

Kate lives in Austin with her husband, cat, dog, and growing family. They love taking full advantage of outdoor activities, hike and bike trails, and the exceptional cuisine Austin has to offer.

PREFACE

Hello,

We would like to thank you for buying our book, *Heart Attack, Cardiac Cath, and Bypass: A Nurse's Guide to Caring for the Patient.*

We have spent a combined 20 years working in many different nursing disciplines. During this time, we have trained hundreds of nurses. We have taken the knowledge and stories we have shared with them and written a book to share with all nurses. We hope that this book provides a simple and easy-to-understand guide to caring for your patients.

The intended audience for this book is nursing students, graduate nurses, and nurses who are new to caring for cardiac patients. The information is explained in a simplified and easy-to-understand manner.

Please visit our website to find out more information about Nurseology and the products we provide. And please feel free to provide feedback or suggestions to info@nurseology.com.

Enjoy!

Jill and Kate

1

ANATOMY AND PHYSIOLOGY

The heart is an amazing muscle responsible for so many important functions of the body. As you already know, the heart is responsible for pumping blood through the entire body, including the brain and other vital organs, and must work well to achieve good health. What happens when the heart doesn't work effectively? How does this impact the patients you care for? Let's talk about the anatomy and physiology of the heart.

The heart muscle contracts and relaxes to move blood through the circulatory system. To do this, the muscle must have an ample oxygen supply, which it gets through the coronary arteries.

The Coronary Arteries
The left main coronary artery supplies blood to the left side of the heart. It has two branches:
1. Circumflex artery: supplies blood to the left atrium.
2. Left anterior descending artery ("the widow maker"): supplies blood to the left ventricle.
The right coronary artery supplies blood to the right atrium and ventricle.

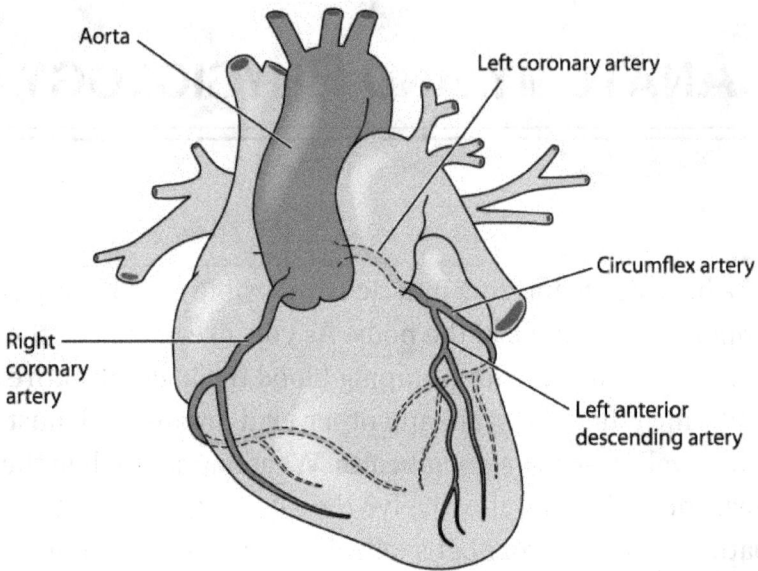

Figure 1: The Coronary Arteries

The Anatomy of the Heart

Thinking of this in terms of a complete cycle will allow you to imagine the entire journey blood takes through the body and how important it is that every part works well and works together to achieve proper function. Let's take a closer look inside the heart and talk about what each part is responsible for.

The inside of the heart is divided into right and left sides. The right side of the heart carries low-oxygenated blood to the lungs where the blood becomes oxygenated and moves into the left side of the heart. From here, the left side of the heart pumps the newly oxygenated blood to the rest of the body where tissues and organs can use the oxygen. The oxygen-depleted blood then makes its way back to the right side of the heart to begin the cycle again.

The right and left sides of the heart are further separated into chambers known as the atria (upper) and ventricles (lower). Valves connect these chambers and open and close to help move blood into the next chamber and avoid backflow into the previous chamber.

Now, let's talk more specifically about each individual part to get a better understanding of how blood travels through each of them on its journey through the body.

The Cycle
Superior and inferior vena cava carry poorly oxygenated blood from the upper and lower parts of the body to the right side of the heart into the right atrium.

⬇

Right atrium pumps the blood received from the superior and inferior vena cava into the right ventricle via the tricuspid valve.

⬇

Tricuspid valve is the first valve in the cycle that allows blood to flow from the right atrium to the right ventricle. It also keeps blood from flowing back into the right atrium.

⬇

Right ventricle is responsible for pumping the poorly oxygenated blood received from the right atrium through the pulmonary valve.

⬇

Pulmonary valve allows the blood pumped from the right ventricle to move into the pulmonary artery.

Pulmonary artery is the pathway for blood received from the right side of the heart into the lungs where it receives its oxygen.

Pulmonary veins from the lungs transport the newly oxygenated blood through these veins and into the left atrium. Don't let this confuse you; this is where veins actually carry oxygenated blood.

Left atrium receives oxygenated blood from the pulmonary veins and carries it through the mitral valve, also known as the bicuspid valve, and into the left ventricle.

Mitral (bicuspid) valve keeps the flow of the blood moving to the left ventricle from the left atrium. One way to remember that blood flows through the tricuspid valve before the bicuspid valve is that when you are purchasing clothes, you always want to "try before you buy."

Left ventricle pumps oxygenated blood through the aortic valve.

Aortic valve allows the blood from the left ventricle to flow into the aorta and prevents it from flowing back into the left ventricle.

⬇

Aorta supplies the newly oxygenated blood from the left ventricle to the rest of the body.

To Review
As blood enters the right side of the heart with the beginning of a contraction, oxygenated blood leaves the left side. The atria contact together, and the ventricles contract together. This is where the "lub dub" sound comes from that you hear when listening to a heartbeat.

The Electricity of the Heart
There is also an electrical component to the heart that causes the muscle to contract in order to move blood through the body.

A special set of cells in the upper heart near the atria—known as nodes—sends out electrical signals to the atria letting them know when to contract. These signals are sent along the same pathway that blood is sent through the structures of the heart. In the ventricles, similar electrical pathways—known as bundle branches—carry the signal through the ventricles allowing them to contract.

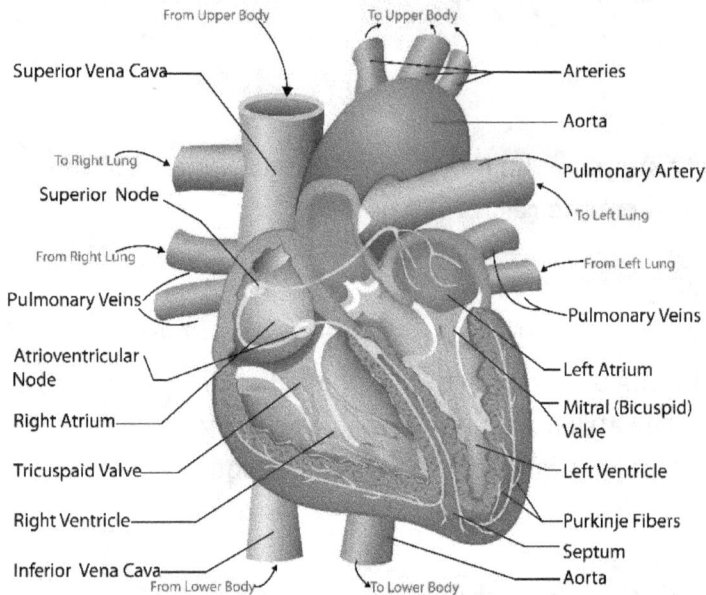

Figure 2: The Structures of the Heart

Nodes

- Sinoatrial (SA) node sets the pace of the heartbeat.
- Atrioventricular (AV) node receives the signal from the atria and channels the signal to the ventricles. This signal is known as the gateway between the atria and ventricles.

Bundle Branches

- Carry the signal through the ventricle walls.
- The ventricle squeezes along with this signal.
- A block on either side of these branches will affect how the ventricles contract.

Purkinje Fibers

The right and left bundle branches divide into smaller branches creating a network of fibers that reaches the ventricular muscle and all the way down to the apex of the heart.

Bundle Branch Blocks

Right Bundle Branch Block

Right bundle branch block occurs when the right bundle branch does not conduct electricity and the signal from the atria reaches the ventricles only by way of the left bundle branch. This causes the right ventricle to have a delayed squeeze.

Left Bundle Branch Block

With a left bundle branch block, the signal is slowed and does not reach the ventricle as fast as it should. This causes the left ventricle to squeeze later.

Cardiac Rhythms

We've already discussed how the heart has both mechanical and electrical functions. Let's dive a little more into the actual rhythms you might see on a cardiac monitor.

When you see a waveform on a monitor, look for the following components:

- P wave.
- QRS complex.
- T wave.
- U wave.

We could write a whole separate book on how to interpret the size and presentation of these waves, but for now, we will stick with the basics.

Cardiac Rhythms
Following is a list of common rhythms associated with heart attack. It is not all inclusive of all dysrhythmias, so be sure to familiarize yourself with the others, such as atrial fibrillation, atrial flutter, junctional rhythms, and AV blocks.

Sinus Rhythm
- Normal heart rhythm.
- 60–100 bmp.

Sinus Bradycardia
- Slow sinus rhythm.
- SA node is firing at a slower rate.
- < 60 bpm.

Sinus Tachycardia
- Fast sinus rhythm.
- > 100 bpm.

Supraventricular Tachycardia (SVT)
- Fast rhythm, >100, and can be faster than 200 bmp.
- Signal may not come from SA node, but rather AV node.
- Several types of SVT.

Premature Ventricular Contractions (PVC)
- Premature firing from the ventricle, not the SA node.
- Commonly feels like a skipped beat or "flopping" in the chest.
- Typically harmless.

Ventricular Tachycardia (VT or V Tach)
- When 3 or more PVC's happen in a row at a rate faster than 100 bpm.
- If < 30 seconds, nonsustained VT.
- If > 30 seconds, sustained VT.
- Monomorphic and polymorphic types.
- Can have with or without pulse. Check for this!

Ventricular Fibrillation
- Begins in the ventricles.
- Chaotic, lethal rhythm.
- Heart muscle "quivers."
- No pulse will be present.
- Must defibrillate.

Asystole
- Cardiac standstill.
- Complete absence of ventricular activity.
- No pulse, no rhythm.

Key Point
Be aware of pulseless electrical activity (PEA). You may see what looks like a rhythm on the monitor, but the patient will not have a pulse. Be sure to always check for a pulse!

2
ASSESSMENT

Every year, more than 600,000 people die of heart disease in the United States. It is the leading cause of death for both men and women, accounting for 1 in 4 deaths. Annually, approximately 735,000 Americans have a heart attack.

Risk Factors
- High blood pressure.
- High cholesterol.
- Smoking.
- Diabetes.
- Obesity.
- Poor diet.
- Low physical activity.
- Excessive alcohol use.

It is crucial to educate patients who are at risk for or have already had a heart attack on both risk factors and signs and symptoms of a heart attack.

When the ability of blood vessels to provide oxygen for the heart is diminished, the heart tissue begins to die. This can be caused by inadequate oxygen supply caused by anemia, hypoxemia, or a clot. It can also be caused by an increase in the heart's oxygen demand from exercise, smoking, congestive heart failure, stress, drugs, or hypertension.

Symptoms of a Heart Attack

- Pressure, squeezing, burning, fullness, or tightness in the chest. Often described as an elephant sitting on the patient's chest.
- Pain or discomfort in one or both arms, jaw, neck, back, or even stomach.
- Shortness of breath.
- Diaphoresis (sweating).
- Nausea.
- Lightheadedness.

Assessment

In nursing, you know the importance of assessment. It is what you were trained to do and it is how you plan the care of your patients. In terms of a patient with a cardiac issue, what things do you want to focus on?

If your patient complains of chest pain, you want to be sure to start with the basics and begin critically thinking about what is causing this pain.

Here's what to assess first:
- Vital signs.
- Electrocardiogram (ECG or EKG).
- Heart and lung sounds.

At this time, be sure to explain to your patient what you are doing and why. This is likely a scary time for the patient, so you want to reassure her that you are on top of it!

What else do you want to look for during this initial assessment period? How does your patient look? Is he pale, sweating, or in severe pain?

This would also be a good time to consider giving your patient some extra oxygen. If the patient is, in fact, having a heart attack, you want to help her body perfuse all of her tissues as much as possible. Start with 2–4L of oxygen via nasal cannula, and increase as needed. Make sure your patient has a working IV. (We'll talk more about nursing interventions in the next chapter.)

EKG
While waiting for the EKG, you know now to start your assessment.

Is this, in fact, a cardiac event? Is it unstable angina? Is it a non-ST elevation myocardial infarction (NSTEMI)? Or is it, in fact, an ST elevation myocardial infarction (STEMI)?

ST Elevated Myocardial Infarction (STEMI)

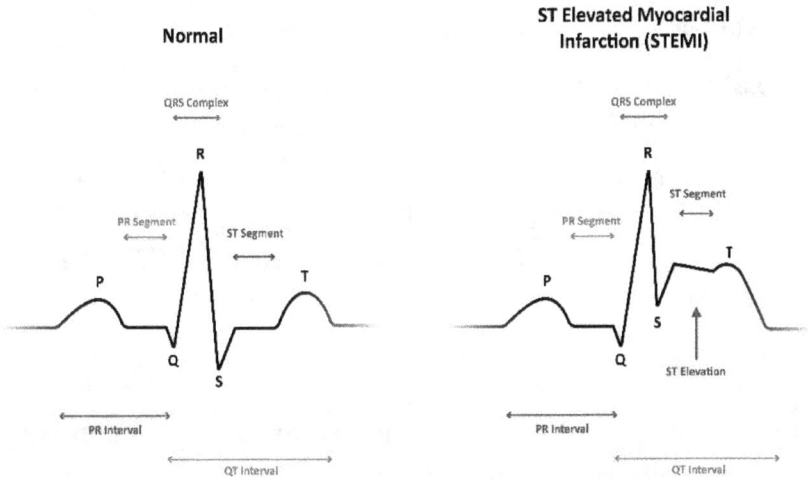

Figure 3: Illustration of an EKG Reading of a STEMI

The location of the STEMI can be determined just by looking at the EKG (Table 1). This is a great diagnostic tool. Even though a cardiologist should have the final say in interpreting the EKG, it is a skill that any nurse who cares for cardiac patients should acquire.

| **Nursing Guidelines** |
| A STEMI is an emergency, and activation of the cath lab team should happen immediately! Remember—time is heart muscle! Even the shortest delay can increase the risk of mortality. |

Table 1 mimics the layout of an actual EKG. If you compare your patient's ST elevation on the EKG to the location in

Table 1, you can determine where the infarct is happening in the patient's heart and which vessel may be blocked.

Table 1: Layout of an EKG			
I Lateral Circumflex artery	**aVR**	**V1 Septal** Left anterior descending artery	**V4 Anterior** Right coronary artery
II Inferior Right coronary artery	**aVL Lateral** Circumflex artery	**V2 Septal** Left anterior descending artery	**V5 Lateral** Circumflex artery
III Inferior Right coronary artery	**aVF Inferior** Right coronary artery	**V3 Anterior** Right coronary artery	**V6 Lateral** Circumflex artery

Lab values will provide crucial information to you and the doctor. Cardiac enzymes, electrolytes, and other labs will help guide the plan of care should any of them be abnormal. Anticipate that these will be ordered.

Cardiac Enzymes
Cardiac enzymes measure specific enzymes and proteins in the blood that are associated with injury to the heart muscle. The cardiac enzyme group is made up of the enzyme creatine kinase (CK) and the proteins troponin I and troponin T. A more specific kind of creatine kinase, called creatine kinase myoglobin (CK-MB), which is found in both heart and skeletal muscle, can be detected earlier than the other

enzymes. This is because it leaks out of the heart more rapidly when heart muscle has experienced an infarct.

Normally, cardiac enzymes are found in low levels in the bloodstream. But as mentioned before, if the heart muscle is injured, the enzymes and proteins leak out of damaged heart muscle cells, and the levels become elevated in the blood. Table 2 explains the onset, peak, and duration of each of the cardiac enzymes.

Table 2: The Cardiac Enzymes			
Test	Onset	Peak	Duration
Troponin	2–6 hours	24–48 hours	4–14 days
CK	3–12 hours	24 hours	2–4 days
CK-MB	3–12 hours	24 hours	2–4 days

3

INITIAL TREATMENT

OK, we have learned the basics, so let's talk about what you and your team need to do. The most important thing to keep in the back of your mind is that *time is heart muscle!* The longer it takes the patient to get treatment, the longer that blockage is preventing oxygen-rich blood from pumping to the vital heart muscle. So everything you do next can determine the patient's outcome.

Your patient has developed chest pain. What do you do next?

This scenario can play out in a couple of different ways:
- Your patient calls 911, EMS responds, and brings the patient to the ED.
- Your patient is already in the hospital and develops chest pain while you are the caregiver.

Regardless of where this process begins, the following steps are vital:
- Check the patient's vital signs. Look for significant changes.
- Obtain an EKG. Look for ST elevation. Compare an old EKG to the new one, and look for changes.
- Place the patient on oxygen, 2–4L nasal cannula, to maintain an oxygen saturation > 92%.

- Call the physician. Some hospitals have policies that allow the nursing staff to administer basic chest pain protocol orders while waiting for a physician to call back. Check with your facility to see what is allowed.
- Activate the cath lab team.
- Administer one tab of nitroglycerin (nitro) sublingual. This vasodilator will help to open up the venous and arterial blood supply. It reduces the workload on the heart, thereby reducing myocardial oxygen demand. Nitro can cause hypotension, so monitor your patient closely. It should not be given if the patient's SBP < 90. You may repeat the dose 2 more times every 5 minutes if the blood pressure remains stable. Some patients will report almost instant improvement after receiving nitro.
- Let your charge nurse know what is going on. This process should all be happening very quickly, so a second set of hands will help expedite everything. Also, if the patient's condition continues to decline, you will have help readily available without having to go into the details of what's been happening.
- Establish IV access. You should always have a working IV whenever your patient's condition is worsening. You never know what could happen next.
- Administer morphine IV 2–4mg. It can help to further reduce chest pain and the patient's anxiety.
- Administer aspirin 325mg. Have your patient chew it for faster absorption. It can help prevent the clot from further forming by inhibiting platelet aggregation.

- Draw cardiac enzymes.

Remember MONA, the acronym from nursing school? MONA greets all patients: Morphine, Oxygen, Nitro, Aspirin. We didn't list it in that order because, realistically, that isn't exactly how it happens.

If you are an emergency department nurse, then most of these tasks have probably been completed by EMS.

Now, to the next phase. You have completed these interventions. But the work doesn't stop there. Something needs to be done to remove the blockage.

If it is an ST elevation MI, you have two options:
1. Take the patient to the cath lab to have a stent placed or an angioplasty done (most common).
2. Administer fibrinolytics to dissolve the clot (least common).

These actions are very time sensitive and should be done as quickly as possible. Research has shown that the best outcomes and patient mortality rates occur when the patient is taken to the cath lab. However, depending on the hospital or location of the hospital, that is not always an option. (You can read about heart caths in detail in the next chapter.)

Fibrinolytics
- This is an IV pharmacological method of reperfusion.
- Usually given over an hour.
- Goal for "door-to-needle" time is 30 minutes.

- Can be given in most hospital settings.
- The patient should be transferred to a hospital capable of performing a cardiac cath after receiving fibrinolytics.

4
CARDIAC CATH

Cardiac cath—also referred to as percutaneous coronary intervention (PCI) or heart cath—is a procedure done under moderate sedation in which a catheter is guided through the body and into the heart to open a blockage in the coronary arteries.

> **Key Point**
> For STEMI patients, the goal for "door-to-balloon" time is 60 to 90 minutes.

Precath Care and Orders

Not all patients will require an emergent heart cath. These orders vary, depending on the circumstances related to why the patient is having the cath, but the following always apply:

- Consents must always be signed unless it is determined to be an emergency life-saving procedure and the patient is unable to sign. Most doctors also require a consent for an emergent bypass.
- Patent IV.
- NPO after midnight.
- EKG within 48 hours of the cath.
- Labs:
  - CBC.
  - BMP.

- PT/INR.

All of these are standard labs ordered to establish a baseline and look for any abnormal values.

A basic metabolic panel, or BMP, includes a creatinine level, which is important to establish the patient's baseline kidney function. The contrast given during the procedure can impair the kidneys. The doctor can trend this value from preprocedure and postprocedure to make sure there was no negative effect on the kidneys.

A PT/INR looks at how thin the patient's blood is. If the patient is on blood thinners, such as warfarin (Coumadin) or enoxaparin (Lovenox), then the patient may be prone to bleeding easier. This could lead to problems with bleeding from the incision site postprocedure.

- Hold enoxaparin the morning of the procedure, as per the orders.
- Hold or modify doses of insulin to account for the NPO status, as per the orders.
- IV fluids: NS or ½ NS may be started to help hydrate the patient and flush the kidneys.
- Have the patient void before leaving for the cath lab. The patient will receive a large amount of IV fluids intraprocedure and postprocedure and will be on bedrest for a while following.

The Procedure
During this procedure, the patient is placed under moderate sedation, most likely versed and fentanyl. Once the patient is relaxed and in place, the doctor numbs an area and makes a tiny incision to insert a catheter into the artery. Sites most often used are the femoral or radial

29

arteries. Using fluoroscopy or continuous X-rays, the doctor guides this catheter up to the heart and injects contrast to view the blood flow through the coronary arteries. (See Figure 4.)

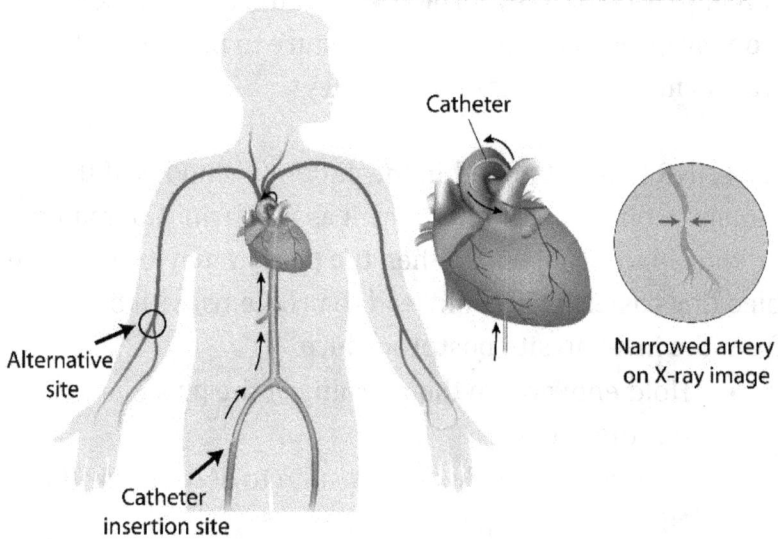

Cardiac Catheterization

Catheter

Alternative site

Catheter insertion site

Narrowed artery on X-ray image

Figure 4: Path of Catheter During Cardiac Catheterization

If a blockage is noted, then the doctor attempts to open the vessel by performing angioplasty or placing a stent (Figure 5). In some cases, this procedure is done for diagnostic purposes, and no intervention is performed. If the patient's blockage is too severe or too complex for stents or angioplasty, then a bypass may be recommended.

ANGIOPLASTY

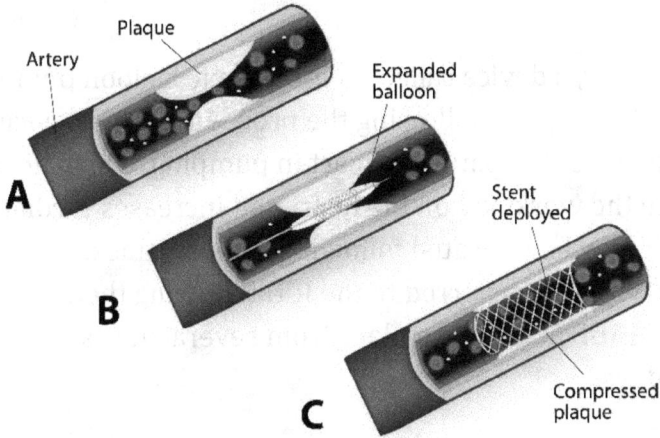

Figure 5: Steps in Angioplasty

During the procedure, the patient may receive blood thinning or platelet-inhibiting products that help to prevent any clots from forming while the procedure is in progress. They may also help to keep new stents patent. These drugs are abciximab (ReoPro), eptifibatide (Integrilin), bivalirudin (Angiomax), or enoxaparin (Lovenox).

The procedure itself can take anywhere from 20 to 60 minutes, depending on what is being done. If the patient is having stents placed, then the procedure will take longer.

After the procedure, the doctor removes the catheter. A sheath, which looks similar to a giant IV or central line, remains in place at the insertion site. The sheath is used as an introducer for the catheters that are passed up to the heart. Think of it as a large tube that holds the artery open while the doctor performs the cath. It is usually sewn in place.

In some cases, a device called an intraaortic balloon pump (IABP) is left in place following the procedure. This device is used to assist the patient's heart in pumping, which helps to reduce the workload on the heart and increases cardiac output. It may be indicated following a heart attack. These patients will be transferred to the ICU following their heart cath. The IABP may stay in place from several hours to several days.

 Removing the sheath may be done by the cath lab team after the procedure is completed. This most often occurs when no intervention was performed. Alternatively, the sheath may remain in place for 4 to 6 hours after the procedure is completed. This allows time for any blood-thinning products given intraprocedure to wear off.

There are various methods to sealing off the artery after the sheath is removed:
- Angio-seal: a collagen plug that is deployed at the sheath insertion site. It is placed by the doctor when the procedure is over and the sheath is removed. This tiny plug is made of collagen and remains in place indefinitely. It is naturally absorbed by the body as the site heals.
- FemoStop or TR Band: a pressure device that applies a set amount of pressure on the site to counteract the pressure of the artery. It prevents bleeding and allows the site to achieve hemostasis.

The nurse will gradually reduce the pressure that is applied and eventually remove it.

- Manual pressure may be applied after the sheath is removed. This may be done in the cath lab or by a trained nurse. (This method will be discussed in further detail in the following section.)

Postcath Care and Orders

You are the nurse who will be receiving the postcath patient. What's next?

What you should find out in the report:

- Presentation: STEMI, positive stress test, positive cardiac enzymes.
- Interventions performed: stents, angioplasty.
- Vital signs.
- Sedation: medications and doses.
- Any complications.
- Special instructions.
- Sheaths: removed, time of hemostasis, how long bedrest is, when sheath should be removed.

Femoral Approach

Bedrest

The patient arrives lying flat on their back if the cath team used a femoral approach. Bedrest is one of the biggest parts of getting through the next 12 hours with your patient. No matter what was done during the procedure, the patient will have to lie flat on bedrest for up to 8 hours or more. Patients who have back or respiratory problems have a difficult time staying flat. Patients must eat and use the bedpan to void lying flat. Bedrest is not a pleasant experience.

The femoral artery is a high-pressure vessel. If any stress or added pressure is placed on that site, it can develop a hematoma or bleed. Remember that the doctor made the small incision in the groin to access that artery. Think about if you kinked a water hose and poked a hole in it, water would spray out. The artery acts in the same manner. (Well, that might be a little bit of a dramatic description, but you get the idea.)

As soon as your patient arrives, instruct the patient and visitors on bedrest:

- Stay flat. (Some doctors may allow the head of the bed to be 30 degrees.)
- If you need to cough, hold pressure on the site to counteract the pressure you are creating by coughing.
- If you need to reposition, you may move or bend the unaffected leg.
- The staff may help you reposition slightly on your side with a pillow for relief from back pain.
- If you feel wetness, warmth, swelling, or pain in the groin area, call immediately.
- I will be in to frequently monitor your site.
- You must use a bedpan and eat while flat on your back.
- Order food that is easy to eat while lying down.
- Always call for help.
- DO NOT GET UP!

Sheath Care

If the sheath has been removed, the site will have a gauze and a Tegaderm in place. The site should be soft and nontender with little to no bruising.

If the sheath is in place, it will be sutured in with gauze and a Tegaderm over the site. The site may ooze, especially if the patient is receiving blood thinners during the procedure. Mild oozing is acceptable and should be manageable.

The sheath may be connected to arterial pressure lines, which you can connect and use to monitor your patient's blood pressure during her bedrest.

Sheath Removal

The doctor will write an order for when the sheath is to be removed. Before you remove it, gather your supplies:

- Suture removal kit.
- Gauze.
- Tegaderm.
- Sterile gloves.
- Atropine.
- 1L normal saline.
- Fentanyl.

You may want to have the patient empty her bladder before removal because you will be holding pressure for a while. (You may want to do the same thing because you won't be able to leave the room.)

If possible, it is helpful to have a second person in the room to assist when you initially remove the sheath. At the very least, let your charge nurse or those working around you know what you are doing in case you need to call them in for help.

Following are the steps for removing the sheath:
- Explain the procedure and plan to the patient.
- Remove and close off any arterial pressure monitors.
- Premedicate with pain medication.
- Place the call light on the bed and within reach.
- Set your monitor to take the patient's blood pressure every 3 minutes.
- Locate and mark a pedal pulse on the foot of the affected leg.
- Don sterile gloves.
- Trim and remove the sutures.
- Feel for a pulse just above the insertion site.
- With a few gauzes placed over the insertion site and on the pulse, carefully remove the sheath.
- Immediately apply a moderate amount of pressure to this site using two or three fingers. You can place your other hand on top of those fingers to add pressure.
- Occasionally use the hand on top to check pedal pulses, and palpate around the site to look for a

hematoma. If you are unable to palpate a pedal pulse, then you may be applying too much pressure.

- Always maintain pressure on the site with one or both hands. ***Never completely remove pressure being held!***
- Monitor the patient's heart rate and blood pressure.
- Continue holding pressure for 20 to 30 minutes.
- You may decrease the amount of pressure being held at the 10-minute mark so long as you maintain hemostasis.
- Once you have developed hemostasis for 20 to 30 minutes, you may release pressure. Palpate around the site to detect hematomas. If any bleeding occurs, continue to hold manual pressure.
- Apply a gauze and a Tegaderm.
- Continue to monitor the groin site every 15 minutes for 1 hour. Then every 30 minutes for 2 hours. Then hourly for 4 hours.
- The doctor will write orders for how long the patient should be on bedrest. Typically, the patient may end bedrest after 4 to 8 hours.
- When bedrest is completed, assist your patient with getting up and walking. Make sure to monitor the groin site during this time, as it will be the first time there is a significant increase in pressure placed on the groin since the procedure.

Complications

Any of the following four complications could occur.

1. *Vasovagal response* occurs when the vagal nerve is stimulated from manual pressure being held. The patient's

heart rate and blood pressure will drop. He may feel faint, nauseous, lightheaded, or dizzy. Give the patient atropine and a fluid bolus. Do not stop holding pressure if this happens. Call for help.

2. *Hematoma* is a collection of blood that develops within the body. If your cath lab patient develops a hematoma, it will usually be around the insertion site. If you are holding manual pressure and a hematoma develops, then you are not holding pressure on the artery. Reposition your hand and add pressure. The patient's blood pressure can drop if the blood loss is significant. You may need to start a normal saline bolus. If the hematoma size is significant, you need to notify the doctor.

3. *Pseudoaneurysm* occurs when the arterial wall is damaged and a blood-filled pocket develops within the lumen. An ultrasound can confirm its presence. You may notice a pulsatile mass near the groin site. The patient may develop hypotension due to blood loss. Start normal saline.

4. *Retroperitoneal hematoma* typically occurs when the arterial stick occurs higher up on the groin. The artery bleeds into the abdominal cavity. Your patient may complain of flank pain and develop hypotension. A CT scan or ultrasound can confirm its presence. Eventually, the patient may develop a large bruise over her flank or abdomen on the affected side, also known as Cullen's sign or Grey Turner's sign.

Radial Approach

If the patient has a radial approach, then his limitations are much less. Some doctors may order bedrest for a short period, but the patient can move around in bed and sit up. These patients will have a TR Band in place. This band applies pressure to the puncture site.

If the patient has a TR Band, do the following:
- Monitor site every 15 minutes for hematoma, bleeding, capillary refill, sensation, and color.
- Begin deflating the cuff after approximately 2 hours.
- Keep the patient in bed during weaning.
- Remove 3mL of air every 5 to 15 minutes. If bleeding occurs, reinject air until bleeding stops. It should take 30 to 60 minutes to completely deflate.
- After the TR Band is removed, apply gauze and a Tegaderm to the site, and monitor for bleeding.
- If bleeding occurs, hold pressure.

Postcath Orders
- Obtain EKG.
- Administer ½ normal saline to help flush contrast used during procedure from kidneys.
- Resume previous diet as tolerated.
- Vital signs: it is important to maintain the patient's blood pressure within a normal range. Remember, you want to avoid anything that puts added pressure on the arterial puncture site. An elevated blood pressure applies pressure to that site from the inside. High blood pressure can cause the site to bleed.

- Echocardiogram: looks at the structure, blood flow of the heart, and ejection fraction (percentage of blood ejected by the heart as it contracts). It can detect the presence of heart failure caused by a heart attack.
- Platelet inhibitors: these may be given intraprocedure or postprocedure to reduce the risk of platelet aggregation and further cardiac ischemia:
  - Plavix.
  - Effient.
  - Aspirin.
  - IV forms discussed earlier in this chapter under "The Procedure" section.
- Patient may shower the next morning following the procedure. Remove gauze and Tegaderm and replace with a bandage, or leave open to air.
- At discharge:
  - Instruct the patient on limiting activity for a week. No heavy lifting greater than 10lbs or strenuous activity. No baths or hot tubs for 1 week. No driving for 1 week.
  - If platelet inhibitors are prescribed at discharge, you must stress the importance of taking these medications as prescribed. If the patient stops taking them, then the stent could occlude.
  - Tell the patient to call 911 if hematoma or significant bleeding develops. Tell the patient to lie down and hold pressure to site.
  - Call immediately for signs of infection.

5
Non-STEMI and Unstable Angina

A non-STEMI is a partial blockage of the coronary arteries that is enough to cause some tissue damage and necrosis. It is less severe than a STEMI, and the symptoms may be milder. The patient will have elevated cardiac enzymes. The EKG will show ST depression with possible T wave inversion. The non-STEMI will not have ST elevation, hence the name.

Unstable angina occurs because of a nonocclusive thrombus within the coronary arteries. The EKG may be normal or abnormal. Cardiac enzymes will be normal.

Orders
- Telemetry: continuously monitor the patient's cardiac rhythm.
- Vital signs: every 4 hours.
- Oxygen: titrate to keep the patient's oxygen saturation above 92%.
- Heart healthy diet or NPO for procedure.
- EKG: on admission, daily, and as needed for chest pain. Look for changes from previous EKG. Call the doctor if there are changes.

- Cardiac enzymes: CK, CK-MB, and troponin. Done on admission and every 8 hours for a total of 3. Call the doctor immediately if elevated.
- Labs:
  - CBC.
  - Lipid profile.
  - Basic.
- Medications:
  - Aspirin and/or clopidogrel (Plavix): these drugs can help inhibit platelet aggregation and further clot formation in the presence of a heart attack.
  - Beta blockers: reduce oxygen demand on the heart by slowing the heart rate, blood pressure, and contractility. Studies have shown a reduction in mortality rates when beta blocker therapy has been initiated.
  - Nitroglycerin: may be prescribed as topical paste, IV, or sublingual. This vasodilator helps to open up the venous and arterial blood supply. It reduces the workload on the heart, thereby reducing myocardial oxygen demand. In some cases of persistent chest pain, patients receive nitroglycerin IV. It is titrated to relieve chest pain.
  - Lovenox or heparin: anticoagulation during or after a cardiac event can help prevent further damage. Lovenox is the drug of choice; however, you may still see IV heparin used.
  - Statins: given to patients who have high cholesterol.
  - ACE inhibitors: if heart failure or the ejection fraction is less than 40%, an ACE inhibitor may be ordered. These drugs help relax blood

vessels, which allows the heart to pump more blood without working harder.
- Calcium channel blockers: recommended for ischemic symptoms when beta blockers are not effective or not tolerated.

- Diagnostics:
  - Nuclear stress test: radioactive dye is injected into the patient and images are taken. After this, medication is given to the patient to stress the heart. Dye is injected a second time, and images are taken. A comparison can be made between the first and second set of images to determine how the heart tolerated the stress. Patients may need to avoid taking nitrates and beta blockers before this test.
  - Cardiac catheterization: see chapter 4 for details.
  - Echocardiogram: looks at the structure and blood flow of the heart and ejection fraction (percentage of blood ejected by the heart as it contracts). An EKG can detect the presence of heart failure caused by a heart attack.

- Education and discharge instructions:
  - Medication instructions: it is vital that you stress the importance of taking medications as prescribed. Go over the patient's medication schedule and plan for refilling prescriptions. Assure that the patient (and family, if possible) has a clear understanding of the medications' purpose and side effects before discharge.
  - Smoking cessation: this is a difficult one. Most smokers who come in with chest pain didn't start smoking yesterday. They have heard it before and know the consequences. It may be

helpful to offer them strategies for quitting and get them to understand that smoking has a direct effect on their cardiac problem. Don't talk at them; talk with them about it. Ask them what they think about quitting and if they have tried before.

- Cardiac rehab: this is a specific type of outpatient rehab designed for patients who have had a cardiac event. It is also a great way for the patient to continue to get education on a heart healthy lifestyle after discharge.
- Diabetes management: talk with the patient about her diabetes and make sure she has good control over it. Ensure she is managing her blood sugars and taking her medications as prescribed. If your hospital has a diabetes educator, have that person come to speak to the patient.
- Weight loss, nutrition, and blood pressure management: talk with the patient and his family about the importance of maintaining a heart healthy diet. Ask the patient if he checks his blood pressure at home, and see if he knows what a normal blood pressure is. There are so many opportunities to educate your patient on things that can have such a big impact.

6

BYPASS

A coronary artery bypass graft, or CABG, is a surgical procedure that bypasses a blockage in one or more of the coronary arteries. It is done by taking a vein from another part of the body and connecting it to the blocked artery so that the grafted vein provides a detour for blow flow around the blockage.

Bypass is done in patients who have extensive blockage that cannot be treated with stents. Not all patients are good candidates. They must be healthy enough to endure this complex surgical procedure.

Preoperative Care and Orders
If you are the nurse caring for this patient preoperatively, there is a laundry list of things that must be done. We will assume this patient has been admitted to the hospital for chest pain or a heart attack and it has been determined that she needs a CABG.

- Telemetry: the patient should be on a continuous heart monitor.
- Diet: heart healthy and then NPO after midnight before the surgery.
- Consent for surgery: after the doctor has discussed the procedure with the patient, have the patient sign the consent.

- Medications:
    - Beta blocker: may help to prevent atrial fibrillation in the postoperative period.
- Labs and diagnostics: there is a long list of tests ordered to establish the patient's baseline and to assure that she is healthy enough for surgery:
    - Complete blood count.
    - PT/PTT.
    - Basic metabolic panel.
    - Fasting lipid panel.
    - Hg A1C.
    - Type and cross.
    - Urine analysis.
    - EKG.
    - Chest X-ray.
    - ABGs if patient has COPD or smokes.
    - Nasal screening for MRSA.
- Weigh patient.
- Shower or bed bath the evening before and morning of surgery.
- Incentive spirometer (IS) teaching.
- Patient education: It is very important to teach the patient and his family about what to expect postoperatively:
    - Explain that the patient will be intubated and in the ICU.
    - The goal is to be extubated as soon as the patient can tolerate it.
    - Once extubated, the patient will be expected to get out of bed, stand, and walk often.
    - It is important to shower daily.
    - Frequent IS helps prevent pneumonia.

- Other goals to get discharged are weaning off oxygen, having a bowel movement, and tolerating oral pain medication only.

The Surgery

We already explained the basics earlier so here are the details.

The patient is taken to the operating room. A large incision is made down the center of his chest, and his sternum is sawed open. From there, the heart is exposed.

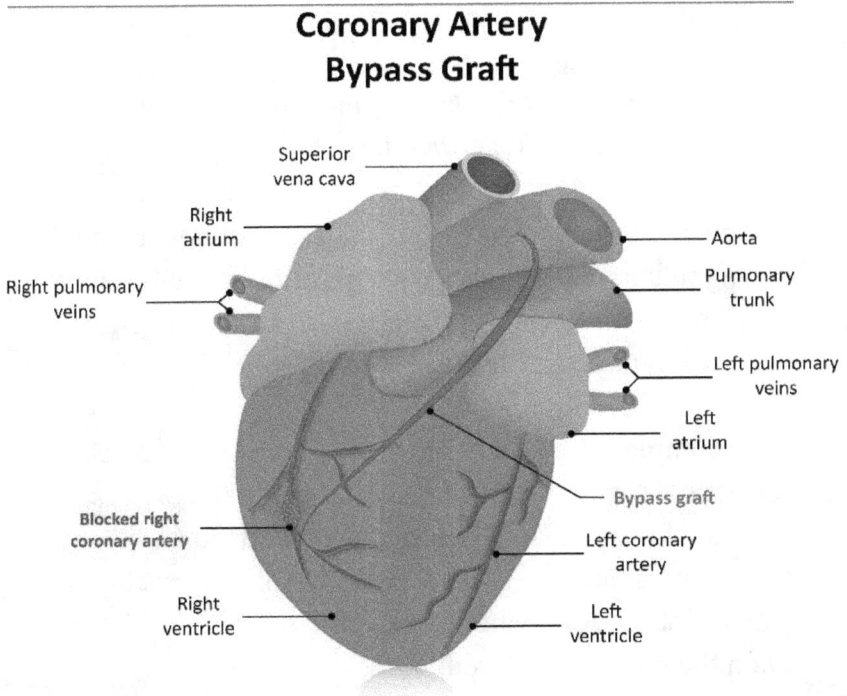

Coronary Artery Bypass Graft

Superior vena cava
Right atrium
Right pulmonary veins
Aorta
Pulmonary trunk
Left pulmonary veins
Left atrium
Bypass graft
Blocked right coronary artery
Left coronary artery
Right ventricle
Left ventricle

Figure 6: CABG for a Blocked Right Coronary Artery

Simultaneously, an assistant performs an endoscopic-assisted vein harvest. The assistant literally tunnels through the legs or other parts of the body looking for veins that can be taken out and used as a graft.

The patient is placed on a bypass machine. A large tube the size of a water hose reroutes the deoxygenated blood from the right atrium to the bypass machine. The machine reoxygenates the blood. Then the machine pumps it back via another water-hose-sized tube into the aorta. The blood is then circulated throughout the body.

> **Interesting Point**
> The patient doesn't have a pulse while on the bypass machine because the machine continuously flows instead of "pumping" as the heart does. Kind of weird, right?

The heart does not beat and blood does not flow through it during this part of the surgery. This allows a stable surgical field for the cardiothoracic surgeon to attach the grafted vein and bypass the blockage.

Once completed, the patient's heart must be shocked to restart it. Ideally, the patient should be on the bypass machine for less than 2 hours. Once restarted and the operation is finishing, chest tubes, drains, and pacing wires may be left in place. The sternum is closed with thick wire. Then the incision is closed.

From the operating room, the patient goes to the ICU and
spends the next day or two, assuming there are no
complications. The patient will be intubated for a period.
But as soon as she is stable enough, the nurse should start
getting the patient out of bed.

Next, the patient transfers to a cardiac stepdown or
telemetry unit. Here comes your part.

Postoperative Care and Orders
- Telemetry: continuous cardiac monitor to watch for
  changes in rhythms.
- Heart healthy diet.
- Incentive spirometer: every hour while awake. This
  helps prevent pneumonia. It's so simple and it really
  works!
- Shower daily: wash over incisions to clean bacteria
  from surgical sites. Make sure the doctor says it's
  OK to shower.
- Walk: walk often and as much as possible. It is one
  of the best things a patient can do post-CABG for
  recovery.
- Blood sugar control: maintaining adequate blood
  sugars is vital to post-CABG care. Studies have
  shown that very tight control of blood sugars
  reduces infection rate and improves overall

mortality. Your patient may not be diabetic but will still have his blood sugars checked and treated.

- Medications:
  - Cardiac medications: your patient may or may not be on a number of cardiac medications for various reasons specific to her care. Regardless of what you are giving, it is always important to review the vital signs before giving cardiac medications to make sure that heart rate and blood pressure are not too low.
  - Antiplatelet medications: given to prevent blood clots from blocking the new graft.
  - Cholesterol-lowering medications: given to stop the progression of plaque buildup in arteries.
  - Pain medications: pain control is important. If your patient is in pain, she won't want to participate in her therapy and recovery. But the same will occur if she is oversedated on pain medication. Find a routine that allows the patient's pain to be acceptable so that she is willing to participate in her daily care. The goal should be to get the patient on oral medication as soon as possible if her pain is at a tolerable level. If the pain is out of control, call the doctor to change medications.
- Chest tube: patients typically come out of the operating room with a chest tube in. If the output is minimal, it will be removed before transferring out of the ICU. Occasionally, the doctor leaves the tube in place for a longer time. Make sure you assess the insertion site and the collection system thoroughly.
- Pacing wires: these wires are attached to the epicardium and exit through a surgical incision on

the chest. The doctor can connect the wires to an external pacemaker in the event of severe bradycardia. Eventually, the surgeon will remove the wires, but while in place, they should be coiled, capped, and taped to the body. Wear gloves when handling the wires to avoid any electrical current that can transfer from you to the wires.

- Education and discharge instructions:
  - Call 911 for chest pain, fast heartbeat, fluttering in the chest, and feeling faint.
  - Call the doctor for signs of infection (pain, swelling, redness, drainage, and fever); persistent cough; and coughing up colored mucus.
  - Teach the patient how to check his pulse. Instruct him on what is normal and abnormal. Call the doctor if abnormal.
  - Daily weights: educate your patient on fluid retention, and teach her to weigh herself daily. Call the doctor if there is an increase of more than 2 pounds in a day.
  - Exercise: instruct the patient to stay active, not to sit in one spot too long, to take it slow, and to stop if she feels lightheaded or dizzy.
  - Sternum care: it is important to limit upper body activity to allow the sternum to heal. Instruct the patient on how to log roll and use her legs to get out of bed. Never let anyone pull the patient out of bed by her arms. Give the patient a pillow to hold across her chest to help brace the sternum and to keep the patient from accidently using her arms to get up.

- Driving: no driving for 4 to 6 weeks or until the doctor says it is OK.
- Medication instructions: it is vital that you stress the importance of taking medications as prescribed. Go over the patient's medication schedule and plan for refilling prescriptions. Assure that he has a clear understanding of the medications' purpose and side effects before discharge. Instruct him not to stop taking medications unless discussed with his doctor first.
- Smoking cessation: this is a difficult one. Most smokers who come in with chest pain didn't start smoking yesterday. They have heard it before and know the consequences. It may be helpful to offer them strategies for quitting and get them to understand that smoking has a direct effect on their cardiac problem. Don't talk at them; talk with them about it. Ask them what they think about quitting and if they have tried before.
- Cardiac rehab: this is a specific type of outpatient rehab designed for patients who have had a cardiac event. It is also a great way for the patient to continue to get education on a heart healthy lifestyle after her discharge.
- Diabetes management: talk with the patient about his diabetes, and make sure he has it under control. Ensure he is managing his blood sugars and taking his medications as prescribed. If your hospital has a diabetes educator, have that person come to speak to the patient.

- Weight loss, nutrition, and blood pressure management: talk with the patient and her family about the importance of maintaining a heart healthy diet. Ask the patient if she checks her blood pressure at home, and see if she knows what a normal blood pressure is. There are so many opportunities to educate your patient on things that can have such a big impact.

Complications

Here are some common complications following CABG.

- Atrial fibrillation: it is not completely understood why patients who undergo bypass surgery develop AFib, but it is a common complication. If this happens to your patient, obtain an EKG and a set of vital signs, and notify the doctor.
- Pneumonia: performing IS and early ambulation is the most important things you and your patient can do to prevent pneumonia.
- Infection: help your patient to maintain adequate hygiene by showering. Make sure all health care workers use gloves and clean their hands before touching near an incision site. Surgical infections can be very serious and a major setback for the patient's recovery.

There is a long list of possible complications. Here are a few more that we won't go into detail on but that you should be aware of:

- Heart attack.
- Stroke.
- Cognitive dysfunction.

- Acute renal failure.
- Bleeding.
- Sternal wound.
- Leg wound.
- Phrenic nerve damage.
- Pleural effusions.

> **Key Point**
>
> Atrial fibrillation, or AFib, is an irregular heart rhythm. This irregular electrical impulse in the heart causes the atria to quiver instead of completely contract. As a result, blood pools in the atria causing clots to form. If the patient goes back into a normal rhythm, the atria completely squeezes ejecting potential clots into the patient's circulation, which may cause a stroke. This is why most patients who suffer from AFib are on anticoagulants.

7

CASE STUDIES

The following case studies are based on actual patients we have cared for. These are the most memorable patients for one reason or another. We take away from these stories 3 important points:

1. Chart well.
2. Perform thorough assessments.
3. Act fast when there are changes.

Case Study 1

M.C., a 67-year-old female, is brought to the emergency department by her husband after she complained all morning of heartburn not relieved by a series of antacids. M.C. has a history of high blood pressure and elevated cholesterol. She walks 2 miles every day, but recently has had a stomach bug and took a break from walking, as well as from taking her home medications. She has no other symptoms at this time but assures the hospital staff it is simply indigestion from the spicy dinner she ate the night before.

The cardiologist is consulted and examines her. Although her symptoms aren't typical for a heart attack, he orders a cardiac workup, including an EKG. This is all completed within 15 minutes of her arrival to the hospital. After interpreting the 12-lead EKG, the cardiologist notes ST segment elevation in leads II, III, and aVF, suspecting an infarct in the right coronary artery.

Is M.C. a candidate for the cath lab?
Yes. Her diagnostic tests and diagnosis were complete within 15 minutes to her arrival to the hospital. At this time, the cath lab team should be ready to take her for intervention.

Plan of Care
- Immediate transfer to the cath lab for percutaneous intervention. (Consent for heart cath and possible CABG should be obtained prior.)
- Oxygen 2–4L per nasal cannula.
- Pain management with morphine.
- Begin antiplatelet therapy.
- Telemetry.
- Labs: cardiac enzymes, lipids, BMP, CBC, type and screen.
- Bedrest after procedure, as per MD order.
- Possible cardiac rehab.
- Patient and family education!

Case Study 2
R.E., a 47-year-old male with a history of hypertension, wakes up in the middle of the night with alarming chest pressure. He calls 911 and is taken to the hospital by the paramedics. The paramedics treat him with the MONA sequence and perform a 12-lead EKG in the ambulance that shows ST segment elevation in leads I, aVL, V5, and V6 indicating an infarction in the circumflex artery. When R.E. arrives to the hospital, his vital signs are stable, but his

blood pressure is 177/92. His cardiac enzymes are also all elevated in the emergency department.

Is R.E. a candidate for the cath lab?
Yes. His diagnostic tests were completed on the way to the hospital allowing prompt intervention upon arrival. The cath lab team should be ready to receive R.E., as the hospital was notified by EMS they were en route.

Plan of Care
- Immediate transfer to the cath lab for percutaneous intervention. (Consent for heart cath and possible CABG should be obtained prior.)
- Oxygen 2–4L per nasal cannula.
- Pain management with morphine.
- Begin antiplatelet therapy.
- IV blood pressure management (possibly a drip).
- Telemetry.
- Labs: cardiac enzymes, lipids, BMP, CBC, type and screen.
- Bedrest after procedure, as per MD order.
- Possible cardiac rehab.
- Patient and family education!

Case Study 3
O.C., a 74-year-old male with a history of smoking 1 pack of cigarettes per day, hypertension, and high cholesterol, collapsed in the grocery store with crushing chest pain. The store manager called 911, and EMS brought O.C. directly to the emergency department. Upon arrival, it was discovered that O.C. had elevated cardiac enzymes and ST elevation in leads V1, V2, V3, and V4. When taken to the

cath lab, the cardiologist discovered that O.C.'s LAD was 100% occluded and he would need an emergent CABG. Luckily, O.C. was consented for the CABG before being sent to the cath lab, and the cardiothoracic surgeon on call arrived promptly to begin surgery.

Plan of Care
- Cardiac catheterization and consent for CABG already complete.
- Postop CABG care and monitoring in ICU.
- Transfer to cardiac unit when stable.
- Close monitoring of incision site and blood sugars to minimize infection risk.
- Daily showers.
- Frequent ambulation.
- Pain management.
- Cardiac rehab.
- Patient and family education!

CONCLUSION

Hello again,

We want to thank you for purchasing this book! We hope it was an easy-to-understand resource that will help you to better care for your patients.

If you enjoyed this book, we would like to ask you for a favor. Would you be kind enough to leave a review for this book on Amazon? We would greatly appreciate it!

Don't forget to check us out on Facebook, Instagram (@nurse_ology), and Nurseology.com to see what other cool products we offer.

If there is a book topic you would like to see in the future, please email us at info@nurseology.com.

Thank you and good luck!

Jill and Kate

REFERENCES

Centers for Disease Control and Prevention. (2015). *Heart disease facts.* Retrieved from http://www.cdc.gov/heartdisease/facts.htm

www.ingramcontent.com/pod-product-compliance
Lightning Source LLC
Chambersburg PA
CBHW070817280326
41934CB00012B/3208